Crawling in my skin

2nd EDITION

crawling in my skin

2nd EDITION

by
ASHA sudra

2019

crawling in my skin

Thank you community.

Honorable shout outs:

LSiete - cover artist

Lorenz - affirmation artist

Arlene - healing artist

Mike - lunch artist

Janice - edit/format artist

Jaq - forever artist

table of contents

dreams

My dreams are
filled
with
ants.
Inescapable.
Crawling
all
over insecurities
eased in
everyday
nightmares.
Forged together with doubt
despite
structural soundness.
The sounds of silence
surround the absence
of reasoning.

They're
everywhere.
Having
survived
centuries
of
being ignored
without

being   given
a name.
Existence of a feeling
before
foundation.
Existence of a structure
without
design.
Blueprinted into
tangible
emotions
without   gas   to light   its shape.

They're
everywhere.

In
waking
life
they
appear
as if
a
deception
of
inception
infiltrated reality.

Ensued into causally living
amongst
the
yearning
to be
dead

without
realizing
it.

Phantom
legs
tickled
against
confidence
like
shoulders
looked
over
in disbelief.

They're

everywhere.

Sometimes I see them out of the corner of my eye. When I'm staring eye to eye in the mirror, judging. Their ability to capture my attention despite their tiny physical presence reminds me I am not so significant. We're not strong enough to defeat them.

Body of an Ant
(blueprint for destruction)

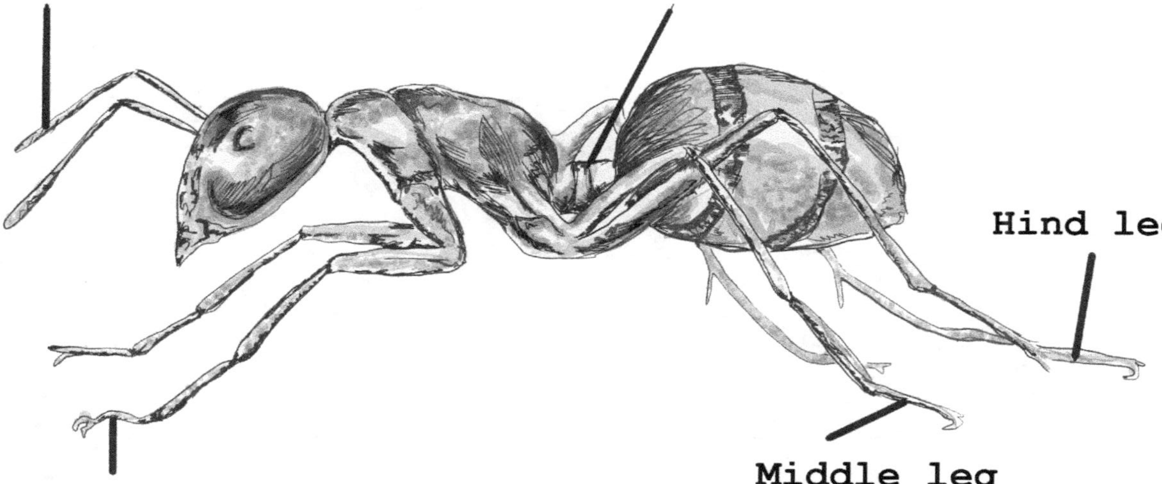

Ants have well-developed antennae. Tasting your insecurities, and smelling your fears
Petioles
Fore leg
Middle leg
Hind leg

Facts about ants / the mind

- There are more than 12,000 species of ants all over the world. 200 classifications of mental illness for 6 legs of decades of running away from truth.

- Ants fight to the death. Their legacy is rooted. They have nothing to prove. You have everything to lose. Proceed with caution. Watch your step.

- Stop screaming. Ants don’t have ears. Ants "hear" by feeling vibrations in the ground through their feet. Carry the weight of emotions with each step knowing you are crushing the doubt beneath you with every waking stride.

- Some queen ants can live for many years and have millions of babies. We are outnumbered by queens. Don’t try to fight it. Unless you’re ready to lose.

- Ants leave a pheromone trail when foraging so they know where they've been. Their scent urges others to follow. To ensure the mission is carried out and structures of self fall. Cleanse. Sage. Repeat.

- An ant can lift 20 times its own body weight. They can knock down giants. Take out tyrants. Ants are unstoppable.

- Ants don't have lungs. They won't let you smoke them out. Self medication is not always the answer. Oxygen enters and carbon dioxide leaves through miniscule holes all over the body. Saturate the air with defense. Hot box.
- When the queen of the colony dies, the colony only survives a few months. Trauma centers in the hurt. Queens are rarely replaced and workers can't reproduce. Don't pick at the scab. Wounds will heal.

One time I got out of the shower, grabbed my towel and wrapped it around me. I looked at the door it was hanging on. It was crawling with ants. Now, my body. Infested.

Camponotus Modoc

Black carpenter ant
dark red legs
indigenous Western North American,
wood working
whittled into existence
making nest in dead wood,
drifted far from self
dead logs
in forests,
amongst trees too tall
to stop to care,
in prevention of stunting growth.

The perfect prey:
human houses
and the brain.
Damaging homes
by nesting in them.
Damaging self

by messing with it.
Doubting its strength.

They will dig out
tunnels
of esteem
in wood to
expand their
living space
leading to
structural damage.
Irreparable damage.

The infestation in the home
a satellite colony,
a cause of systemic malfunction,
a cause of imperialism,
and nutrition,
with the main one within
a hundred yards
or more

in a stump
or other decayed wood.

Watching
keeping an eye on stability
making sure to be quick to
intervene.

When colonies start
to infiltrate,
take back,
establish themselves
in homes,
they may start small
in a few hundred,
but can grow to
tens of thousands.

There can be 20 or more satellite
colonies.
Organized revolution.

I envy organized resistance
even if its against me.

Last night I saw one on the chopping board, in a sink
full of clean dishes.
I haven't seen one in months.
Just when I think it's over.
They ~~used to~~ come out of light sockets
door jams
and cabinets
windowsills
and tone
and attitude
insecurity
and anxiety

Tetramorium caespitum

The pavement ant
native to hate
or
Europe,
also introduced
as an uninvited pest
in North America.
Caucasity.

Colonies in North America
usually making their homes
under pavement.
Under community.
Disrupting the very foundation
we build upon.

It is distinguished
by one pair of spines

on the back,
making it easier to
extend a hug,
convince you of community,
and slice your hands.

During the late spring
and early summer,
colonies attempt to conquer
new areas
and often attack nearby
enemy colonies.
Weaponized toxic emotions.
Killing vibes
and moods
and aesthetics.
This results in huge
sidewalk battles,
household wars
and burned bridges.
sometimes leaving

thousands of ants dead.
Sometimes leaving
just one human.

Because of their
aggressive nature,
they often invade
and colonize
seemingly impenetrable areas
outside their native territory.
Because depression knows no
boundaries
or borders.
Infestation becomes unavoidable.

In summer,
the ants dig out the sand
between the pavements
to vent their nests.
Because even for them,

the emotional toll is

too much to endure,
requiring
distance and
space
to breathe.

Pavement Ant

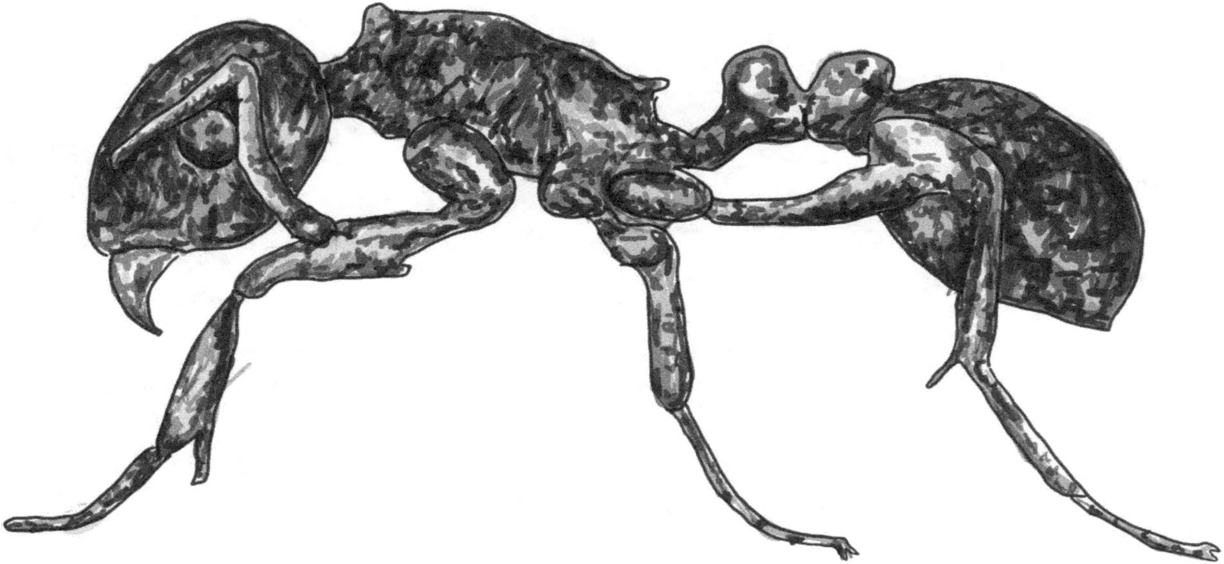

The poison is working.

I haven't seen any traces for a while.

outside my skin

It's like a sixth sense.
    Six silent steps
        marching incognito to a beat only I can
    hear drum
lined in and out of consciousness.
    White noise.

Distraction
    away from reality.
        I sometimes freeze
            staring at them.
        Noticing any peripheral movement of
    doubt
    sinkholed into submission of focus.
Lost.

I can be anywhere
                and
                    notice
                        them.

                    Serene pastures disrupted in
                 one entropic faulty step.

They
    crawl   in my   skin
                                   but   outside
they are building empires.
It's like only I can sense the future.
    This impending doom of
        ant resilience.

    Intuitive reflections of the ways
in which we allow the mind
    to take over
        promise awareness,
            but does not promise preparedness.
        Least expected.
    Least warranted.
Lest we forget the ancestral tools already
gifted.
    Lest we forget who really runs this shit.

Solenopsis molesta

Thief ants,
nesting close to other ant nests,
close to trauma
close to edges
teetering on erosion.
Stealing nourishments.
Stealing will to survive.

Messy
grease ants
attracted to oils
creating grounds too slick to
find confidence.
Too doubtful to trust.

Thief Ant

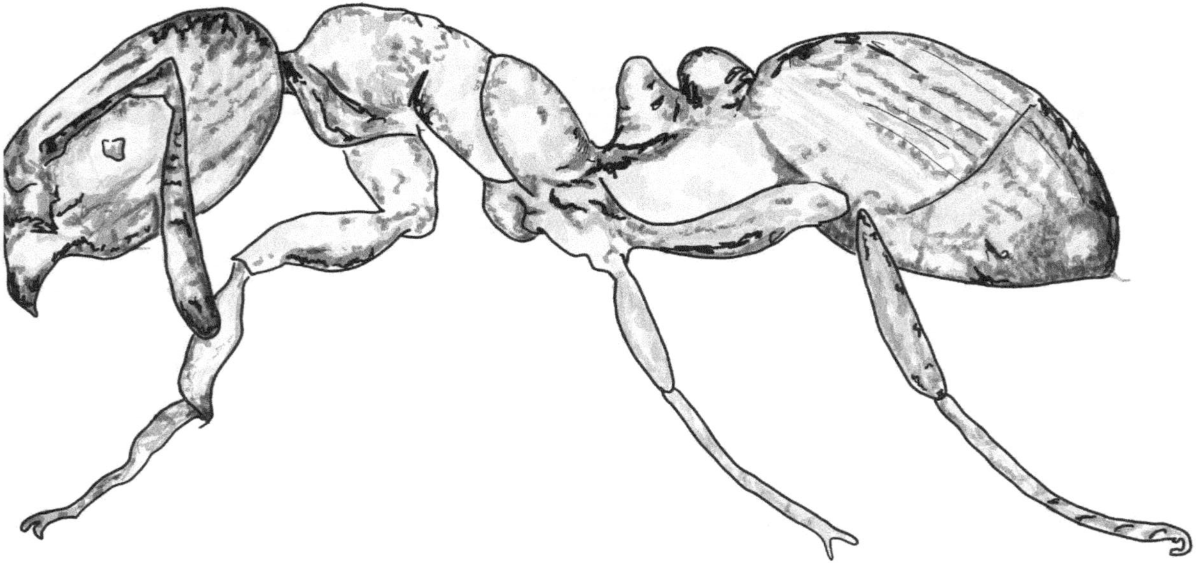

bain of existence

I think the

ants are

getting bigger.

Gothem-citied

into

Bain

existences of

poison

powered up.

Super ants.

They're killing more than just me.

I find bodies all over.

Spiders

once

predator

now poisoned

by

determination.

Now prey to survival.

They hardly take the poison anymore.

They
  know
    to temper
               power
                   and responsibility.
So sure
Of my own self doubt,
They
   don't
       dare
        risk
            ruining the mission.
                       The objective
                           The occupation.

Depression over everything.

crawling in my skin

Learning about yourself is taxing.
The body fatigued
after crossing the id
traversing toxic
environments
and pervasive habits.
Just when thoughts of
cleansed nourishment arise,
mirages of fantasy
dissipate.

Peripheral senses
detect movement
slopes
too steep to prevent slipping.
Progress is jagged.
ebb and flow in moments of
weakness,
it's only natural.

Questioning of self is a trap.
Designed to trick one into opening
unnecessary   gaps
to
allow
                    ants
                        to
nest
in   decay.

I
feel
them   crawling
                        on me

sometimes.
Even though I can't see them,
I know
they   are
                always
                    there.

Legs tickling confidence
to give into holding up feathered
structures.

We are not as strong
as
the
ants.
We do not have the power to fight.
I feel them
around
me.
Living amongst us
in every waking second.
Formication
symptoms solidified
by society
into making me
uncomfortable
in
my
own

skin.
My own self.
Itching to get out for so long.

Until I figured out how to give in.
It changed everything.

Every now and then I find one. Usually near the mirror.
I wonder why they're always around the mirror?

Pheidole

A genus of ants.
Or so assumed.
Self-imposed
and ego driven.
Taking up space just for
acknowledgement.
Dimorphic,
containing two castes of workers.
Duality.

The "minor" workers,
more narrow-minded,
closed off,
lonely.
The "major" workers,
or "soldiers",
enormous heads and mandibles

compared to their

modest

body size.

Gym rats.

They may look fierce,

yet often shy.

Afraid someone will see through

clouded facades

and

often the first to flee

on any hint of danger.

The Big Headed ant

Minor

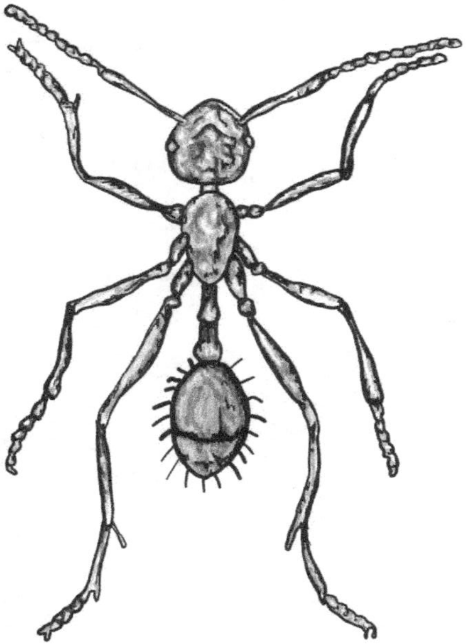

Major

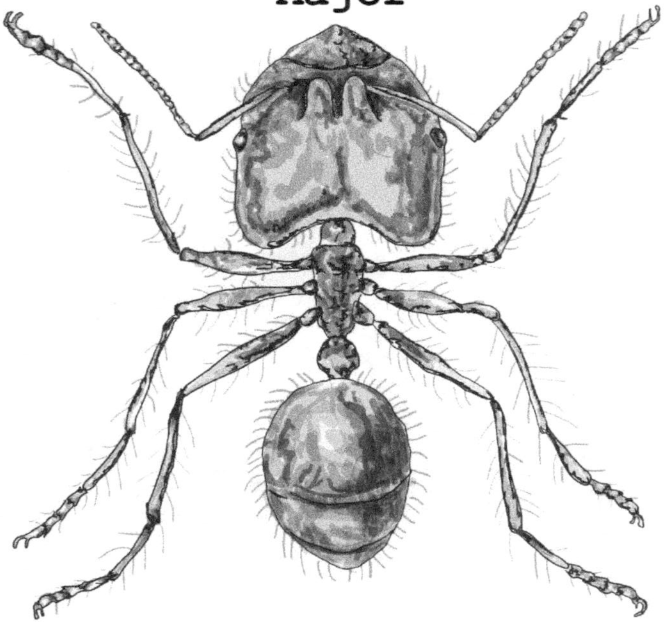

risk it all

I've
seen
them
plummet
great

heights
in attempt to cross

gaps.

I've seen them watch each
other

fall,
and

then

build

bridges.

Holding on to uplift

each other.

Allowing

each one

and the

rest

of the

platoon

to

make

it to

the

other side.

Envious of the camaraderie.

Crawling in isolated thoughts

listening to

drum

like marches

of a

mental

toughness

I never asked for.

insight

I often watch them.
Imagining what they say to each other
each time they pass.

I wonder if they provide insight
to one another.
Updates
on the
mission.
The contingent
stronger
than
ever.

Or to avoid the new
above ground pool
the squad
has
been bathing in.
Rejoicing
in battles won.

Laughing and sharing
stories
of when they scared
me,

or made me scream out in frustration.

I watch them plot my demise in front of me.

I think they do it in front of me because of ego.

My presence a simple tease
Of insecurity
taking over
before my eyes.
Militarized
intel
in quick communication.

Swift execution.

Mobilized mental
Illness destabilization.

Sometimes I think
they see me and laugh.
Knowing
they'll always
win.

Sometimes I think I understand everything
And
sometimes I
don't understand at all.

Tapinoma melanocephalum

Sometimes it goes away.
Sometimes I convince myself
I've killed it
and actually survived.
But at my happiest
I become blind.
Ghost ant.

Dark head
translucent legs.
Floating above stability.
Tricking,
convincing me
that it's smaller than it seems.

Ants are everywhere.
Like depression,
the exact native habitat
is not exactly known.

However, the species
is assumed to originate
in minds from bodies
of brown regions,

The ghost ant
cannot adapt
to colder climates.
It thrives in environments
that are messy,
damp
and musky from anxiety.
They are confined to
greenhouses.
Humid traps of doubt
and buildings
that provide
considerable conditions
that allows the species to thrive,
like gas lit rooms full
of disbelief.

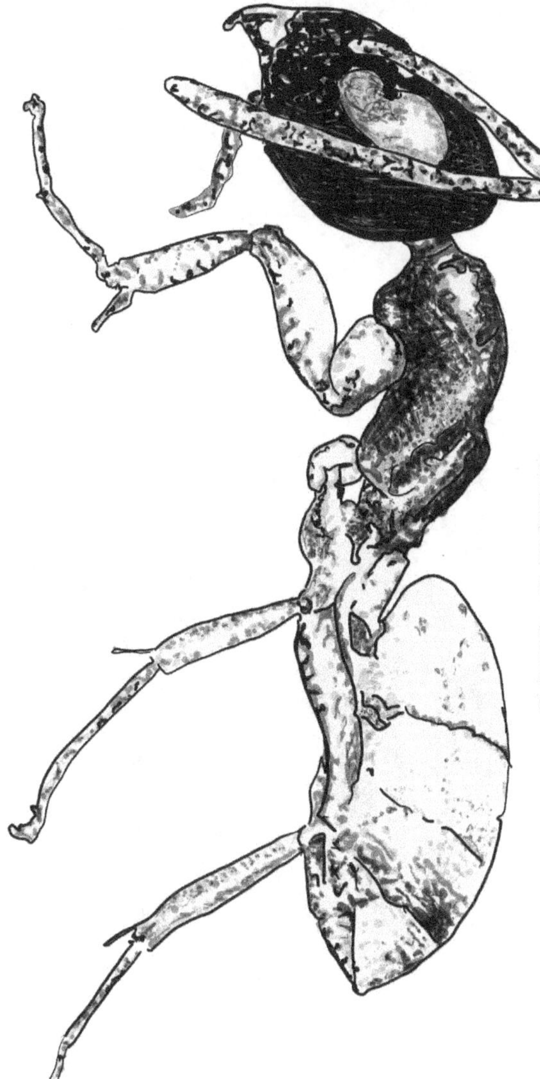

Ghost Ant

I smile now when I see them, knowing they have
reclaimed this territory.
It belongs to them.
I simply exist with-in it.

ants

The ants are back

and

just

like

last month,

and

the month

before that,

and

the

year

before that,

after another month long war

I

think

I can

speak

ant.

Understand

the inner workings

and

deepest thoughts,

and

through extensive field
work
they have told me
they
just want to be
remembered.

Acknowledged

and
not
neglected.

They said
"Structurally claimed driven
mindsets
oppose conditions of being limitless"

and
kind
of
like
this
infestation
of
the
subconscious,
these
war

cries
and tyrant driven
erected monuments
echo
action
of
removing
indigenous
relics
of time
before
darkness.

This
realization triggers
consciousness
trying to avoid ID,

and I

am

the

ego

driven

colonizer.

Suppressing the

reclamation

of space

in pleas for

recognition.

These

ants

speak

a

language

my

body

knows

too well

but refuses to

acknowledge.

I

am

the

dictator

trying

to erase

presence,

their
trail
in
paper
towel
mass graves
and
like
ants
trapped
in bait
I sometimes
bury traces of disease
in eased over formalities
and leave
the effects
lingering
long after
so
as to
deter it
from
returning.

But

since inception
it's always been here.

Exacerbation knowingly

tempting each step
to veer off permitted paths.

The undying
resiliency
of
ants
to reveal their presence
even
amidst
the
most
pristine
the most
perfect
the most desirable
spaces
hold truth
that even those
that are supposed
to
be
without
flaw
have
cracks.

Tiny enough

to seep
in
to
show
there is no place impenetrable
from
the
mind.

The
ants
have
taught
me
acceptance of this structural
manifestation
destines me to forever
be
in
denial.

It might be cleared
out of one
space,

but
it
is
simply

forced
to
move
onto the next.

The reservation
this system
these

ants
rely
on
mirrors the
systematic
depression that plagues
the mind,
like systematic oppression
plagues society.
Hiding
in
crevices
too
small
to
notice,
until
too
late.
Trap

houses
comfort
of
familiarity.

Poison
passed
onto
each
ant in
passing

slowly disseminated throughout
a

colony.

This
chemical
warfare
destroying
evidence of
whatever
or
whoever
occupied
this
land
before.

My cells know this language
these
ants
speak.

They are familiar with
being
ignored
being forced out
being
repressed.

These
week long battles
are
a
reflection
of my
weak-lifelong battle
traveling
through
life
trying to
suppress
chronic
infestation.

Survival sometimes

means to
simply
survive.

But like resistance
of indigenous tribes,
demanding a voice,
and
insects
powerful enough to
stage hostile takeovers
for
being
ignored
far past
comfort contort
conceptions
of self, safety and
community,
Sometimes…

Simple
recognition
goes a long way.

Well,

I've heard what they have to say
and
I
might
give
up
and
just

Let
the
ants win.

Upper View

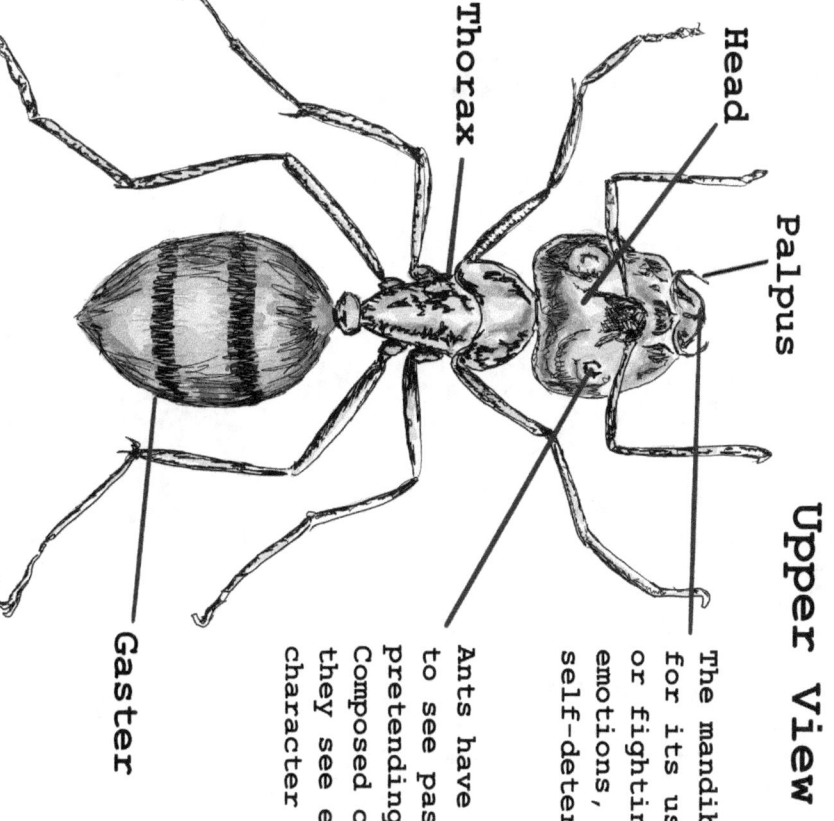

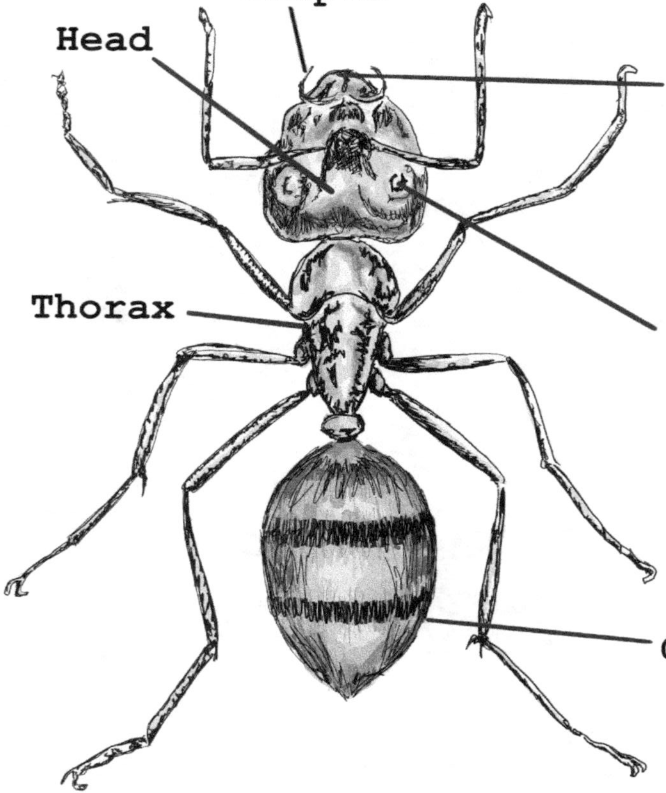
Palpus
Head
Thorax
Gaster

The mandible is very strong for its use in carrying food or fighting with enemies, or emotions, or sense of self-determination

Ants have compound eyes, able to see past fake facades of pretending you're alright. Composed of many tiny eyes, they see every time you break character

the next day

When
you
left
that
morning,
they left the
kitchen.

The light sockets returned to
leveraging electricity
and not mood.
I smiled for hours staring at that corner.
In disbelief and mysticism
questioning day dreamed reality.

It had been
peppered
for
weeks.
Blackened.
Black speckled
granite

linoleum
witness to weakness
and
self
doubt.

And then all of a sudden you showed up.

They still appear
in singles
across
counter tops
countering
super-ego
exaggerations.
Call out
cultured
into
remembering
the infestation
is
forever.
That this
is not over.

But lines once solidified,
broken
into manageable stepping
stones
stressing
tones of maturity.
Of acceptance.
Growth ecosystems
of existence.
Like that one time we went to the party
and spent the whole time laying in bed,
I came home to find a battle I didn't know
I won.
Bodies spilled across counter tops.
Falling to great depths in last wills of
desperation.
I watched them die.
Staring at them for hours.
They flipped
and turned
and attempted any chance to crawl away.
But instead, they would shrivel up.
You made them shrivel up.

You.
    A foreign government supporting an
authoritarian regime
    armed in validation and understanding.
I know
    there are
        still   more.
I know more
        will
            show up somewhere
                new tomorrow and that you might
            not be here.

It’s ok though.

I think it’ll be ok though.

about the author

Originally from LA, ASHA is a multidisciplinary artist and educator in San Jose. She is an intersectional poet, striving to use art to create radical change.

ASHA has been featured on the cover of Content Magazine, as well as the focus of a short documentary by KQED ARTS. She is an active speaker, emcee, and performer at numerous rallies and marches for civil and human rights.

She was given the Hank Hutchins award by the Santa Clara County Alliance of Black Educators, and is actively training teachers across California on equitable practices and building student agency. She has worked with numerous districts and unviersities to talk about Humanizing Education. Her dream is to create a learning space rooted in restorative and social justice.

ASHA consistently uses her platform to voice out against injustice and to speak up for those who have been marginalized and silenced for centuries.

Contact the author:

IG: @asha_poet
contactASHApoet@gmail.com

www.ingramcontent.com/pod-product-compliance
Lightning Source LLC
Chambersburg PA
CBHW051407290426
44108CB00015B/2191
9780578575926